THE "Scarab Club" PAPERS

I

THE TOMBS OF ANCIENT EGYPT

BY

W. L. NASH, F.S.A.

ISBN: 978-1-63923-979-5

All Rights reserved. No part of this book maybe reproduced without written permission from the publishers, except by a reviewer who may quote brief passages in a review to be printed in a newspaper or magazine.

Printed: March 2023

Published and Distributed By:
Lushena Books
607 Country Club Drive, Unit E
Bensenville, IL 60106
www.lushenabks.com

ISBN: 978-1-63923-979-5

IN the following pages I do not pretend to have exhausted the subject of the Egyptian Tomb and its meaning. To do so would require far more space than is at my disposal. But I hope I may have succeeded in interesting those who have perhaps themselves visited the tombs, or have read of them, and desire to know something of the meaning to be attached to the remarkable paintings and sculptures found in them. Numberless are the questions that a consideration of the Tomb gives rise to, and I hope that other Members of "THE SCARAB CLUB" will deal with some of them in a future number of the Club's "Papers".

W. L. NASH.

TOMBS OF ANCIENT EGYPT

To understand the tombs of Ancient Egypt, their arrangement and the scenes painted on the walls, we must realize that the Egyptian's idea of the tomb differed entirely from our own. With us the tomb is the resting-place of the mortal body until, in the course of nature, it shall decay and perish; with the Egyptian it was the depository of the body which they by embalmment endeavoured to preserve from destruction, as they fondly hoped, for ever, and they called it the body's "eternal home". With us the immortal part of man is, at death, freed absolutely from the mortal body; with the Egyptian the two were in constant relationship.

The Egyptians regarded man as composed of different entities, each of which had its separate life and functions.

The more important of these entities were the Ka, the Ab, the Ba, the Khaib, and the Sahu, but it is only the first three of these that especially relate to our subject.

1. THE KA

The Ka was the spiritual counterpart of the deceased; it was his personality, bearing the same relationship to him that a word bears to the idea that it expresses. In the XVIIIth dynasty the personality was not infrequently disjoined from the body. There are many representations illustrating this. In the Temple of Amen, at Luxor, Horus is shown presenting to the god Amen-Ra the infant king Amenhetep III and his Ka; both the Ka and the child are represented as an infant (Fig. 1). Again, there are instances in which the king is shown adoring his own Ka.

The man lived no longer than his Ka remained with him, and it never left him until the moment of death. The Ka could live without the body, but the body could not live without the Ka. Nevertheless, the Ka was not altogether a spiritual body; it was material in the sense that it required food and drink, and if these were denied it it suffered hunger and thirst. In this respect its lot was that of all the Egyptian gods. Moreover, the Ka could

6   TOMBS OF ANCIENT EGYPT

visit the body after death; it could not, however, live without physical support. This support it found sometimes on the body

FIG. 1.

itself, at other times by attaching itself to the statues of the deceased which were placed in the tombs, and often in the Temples, for the purpose. These figures, commonly called "Ka figures", will be referred to later.

2. THE AB

The Ab, or immortal heart, stood in the same relation to the mortal heart as the Ka did to the whole man. It left him at

FIG. 2.

death and travelled through the regions of the other world until it reached the "Abode of Hearts". In the process of embalmment

the heart was removed with the other viscera. But to leave the
body without a heart was to destroy it utterly and so defeat the sole
object of embalming. To avoid this catastrophe an artificial heart
in the form of a scarab was placed on the breast of the mummy.
The scarab or sacred beetle was called "Kheper", which signifies
"become" or "exist", and thus ensured the resurrection to life
after death. On the base of the Heart-scarab is usually engraved
the name of the person with whom it was buried, and also part,
at least, of Chapter XXXB of *The Book of the Dead*, which
contains a prayer that his heart may not be taken from him in the
other world, and that nothing may oppose him at the time of the
great judgment before Osiris, of which I shall give some account
later. The illustration is such a Heart-scarab which was made for
a man named Neb-mes, and his name is engraved in the first line
of the inscription (Fig. 2).

3. THE BA

Of all the immortal parts which combined to make up the man
the Ba seems to come nearest to our idea of a Soul. It was
closely akin to the gods, to whom it flew when death severed its

FIG. 3.

connexion with the body. It is usually represented as a human-
headed bird (Fig. 3). In *The Book of the Dead* is a vignette
depicting the Soul flying down the shaft leading to the mummy
chamber to visit the body in its coffin.

4. THE KHAIB

The Khaib, or shade, which is pictured as a fan (Fig. 3), was
the representative of the Shadow cast by all material objects. It

had a separate existence, and, as we shall see, could undergo punishment.

5. THE SAHU

The Sahu was the ethereal representative of man's *form* on earth. It was a mere empty shell, and thus differed from the Ka, which was a complete personality.

These are the ethereal parts of a man which concern our subject. But although it is usual to speak of them as being separate entities, it is by no means certain that they should not all be regarded as so many phases of the one Ba, or, as we should term it, the Soul. The chief purpose of the daily service in the Temples was to restore to the dead the Soul which had left the body, and without which the man could not live again in the other world. In the ritual of the service no mention is made of the Ka, or of any other of the entities above enumerated, with the exception of the Heart, which was restored together with the Soul. This restoration of the Soul, or Ba, to the dead was typified by the restoration of the Eye of Ra to the image of the god. To the Osirian, death was the work of the evil deity Set, who forced the Soul to leave the body. At the moment of death the Soul flew to the Sun-god Ra and hid itself in either the Solar or Lunar eye of that deity. But Set pursued it to its place of refuge and swallowed the eye of Ra and with it the Soul. At other times he is said to have cast the eye into the Nile. The chief ceremony of the Temple service was the recovery of the eye from the typhonian animal that had swallowed it, or from the waters into which it had been cast. It is, however, impossible to dogmatize on the subject, and for the present purpose it is sufficient to regard the various entities as being separate and distinct from each other.

With these preliminary remarks, necessary to a clear understanding of what follows, but which I fear may prove wearisome to my readers, we may now pass on to the consideration of the tombs themselves.

I do not propose to include the pre-dynastic tombs. They were the outcome of religious ideas which differed altogether from those which prevailed during the dynastic period, and it is to the tombs of this latter period alone that I shall refer.

THE ESSENTIAL PARTS OF A TOMB

However simple or however complex a tomb might be in plan, there were certain parts that were always present in some form or another. The method of providing them, the mode of arranging them, differed at various times, but their presence in some form was invariable. The religious, or rather mythological, ideas of which the tomb was the representation remained unchanged, in general outline at all events, and the tombs therefore must follow the established ritual.

The parts of the tomb which were regarded as essential were—
(1) A central chamber, commonly called the "Chamber of Offerings".
(2) A door provided for the entrance of the Ka.
(3) The Serdab.
(4) The pit, or well, and the burial chamber.

These are the essential parts of every tomb, and in the following pages I propose to describe the use that was made of them.

THE MASTABAS

The earliest monumental tombs are the Mastabas, so called from the resemblance they bear to a bench, the Arab word for which is *mastaba*. They go back to the earliest dynasties, and

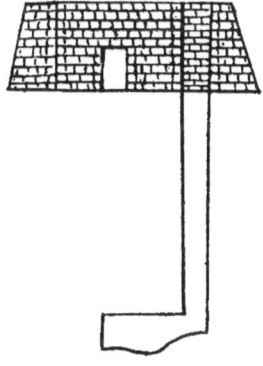

FIG. 4.

cease abruptly at the end of the VIth dynasty. They are found in the necropolis of Memphis between Abû Roash and Dahshûr; at Sakkarah and at Gizeh. Their general shape is oblong, the sides slope symmetrically, and the roof is flat. They are built of stone or of sun-dried bricks. In the former case the interior of the walls is merely rubble, faced on each side with a stone casing. They range in height from 10 to 30 feet or more, and vary greatly in degree of complexity. The illustration (Fig. 4) shows the Mastaba in its simplest form. Those of the Vth and VIth dynasties were greatly enlarged by the addition of numerous chambers grouped round the original simple plan. The building is entered by a doorway that is often devoid of ornamentation. At other times a statue of the deceased was carved on each side of this doorway, and on the lintel, which is cylindrical, were cut his name and titles. The doorway usually leads directly into the chamber.

THE CHAMBER OF OFFERINGS

This chamber was usually of small size, and contained no furniture except a "Table of Offerings". It was intended as a place in which the relatives and friends of the dead could meet for the purpose of making offerings of food for the benefit of his Ka, and also celebrate the funerary sacrifices on the days appointed by law, namely, the "feasts of the commencement of the seasons", i.e., the feast of Thoth on the first day of the new year, the feast of Uaga, the great feast of Sothis, the feast of the procession of the god Min, and many others.

THE KA DOOR

This was a door provided for the passage of the Ka into the tomb and thence into the outer world. Theoretically there were

FIG. 5.

two doors, one for the dead and one for the living. But the former, often called the false door, was nothing but a recess in the wall marked out with side posts and a lintel, formed in the face of the wall looking east. Against it was commonly placed the Stele (Fig. 5), which was a slab of stone usually bearing an invocation to Anubis—a god especially associated with the dead —asking him to ensure abundance of food and all good things to the Ka of the deceased. Below this was usually carved a table,

FIG. 6.

heaped with various foods, at which the dead man is seated. Another example of the Ka door, in this case duplicated, is shown in Fig. 6. Between the two doors are painted scenes of servants bringing materials for the funeral feast which the Ka, represented in the form of the dead man, is enjoying, seated at a table.

THE SERDAB

This was a narrow but lofty niche, or a series of such niches, contrived in the thickness of the wall, usually on the south side. Its only communication with the chamber was by a very narrow slit, barely large enough to admit a man's hand. In it were placed statues of the deceased, which served as supports for the Ka while he benefited by the offerings made to him in the chamber. These figures were intended as, and no doubt often were, portraits of the dead man. They are made of stone or wood, and often are almost the size of life. The Ka was supposed not merely to attach himself to these figures, but to become incorporated with them whenever he desired. So far was this idea carried that the images of the gods in the Temples were regarded as containing their Kas, and were in fact the gods themselves.

THE PIT AND BURIAL CHAMBER

The pit (Fig. 4) was square or oblong in section, never circular. It commenced at the top of the Mastaba, and passed down through the thickness of the wall to a depth of from 40 to 50 feet. It then turned horizontally, and finally was enlarged into a chamber in which the sarcophagus containing the mummy was placed. The horizontal passage was of such a length as to bring the burial chamber vertically under the centre of the floor of the Chamber of Offerings, and so directly beneath the assembled relatives.

THE PYRAMIDS

Contemporaneous with the Mastabas were those vast erections, the Pyramids. They also were tombs—but the tombs of kings, not of subjects. That such was their purpose is clearly seen if we look at a section of one of them, which discloses the internal arrangement of the building. The illustration (Fig. 7) shows a section of the Pyramid of Khufu, the second king of the

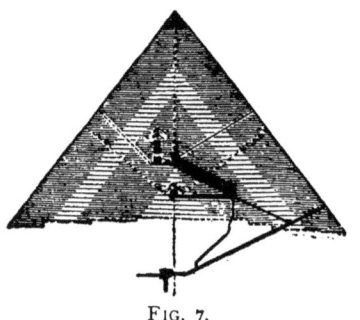

FIG. 7.

IVth dynasty, between 3700 and 4000 B.C. The height of this Pyramid is now about 451 feet, but the apex is broken off and the original height was probably 481 feet. The entrance was on the north side about 43 feet above the ground. From it led a passage 320 feet long, sloping downwards into the solid rock and ending in a chamber which may have originally been intended for the mummy chamber. Just before the passage leaves the built mass of the Pyramid there is a granite door. This seems to have baffled the early tomb-robbers, and they cut a path round it and found themselves in a passage sloping upwards for a distance of

125 feet. At this point a horizontal passage branches off and leads to what is commonly, but erroneously, called the "Queen's Chamber", while the original passage ends in a large sloping hall which led into the "King's Chamber" in which the sarcophagus was found.

The Pyramid, then, was a royal tomb concealed within a gigantic mass of masonry which was faced within and without with slabs of granite. The absence will be noted of any Chamber of Offerings and a Serdab, which were essential parts of a tomb.

From very early times the kings separated the sepulchral chamber from the rest of the tomb. In every case they built what may be described as a "Funerary Temple" outside the tomb, sometimes close to it, at other times a considerable distance from it. The king's body was deposited within the tomb, whether it was a built Pyramid or, as in later times, a rock-cut tomb; the funerary services were performed in the Temple wherein were placed the statues or Ka figures.

From the end of the VIth dynasty until the re-establishment of the monarchy in the XIth dynasty, that is to say, for a period of more than five hundred years, the government of Egypt was in the hands of the numerous tribal chieftains, whom the kings had for years bribed and cajoled into some semblance of obedience to their authority. These chieftains fought among themselves for supremacy, and all united in plundering the people. The confusion into which the whole country fell is reflected in the all but complete absence of monuments of the period.

But with the XIth, and still more with the XIIth dynasty, came a renaissance of Art, and for a time the sculptor, the worker in the precious metals, the potter, and the carver, produced works which, for beauty and for skilful workmanship, have never been surpassed. It is at this period that we may resume the examination of the tombs.

Of the royal tombs of this period we know but little. Like their predecessors the kings erected Pyramids to mark their places of burial, and some of these Pyramids have been identified. That the tombs of many of these kings were known so late as the XXth dynasty is certain, for they appear in the lists of those which were examined by the Ramesside Inspectors, and were found to be intact. But in later times they were plundered and destroyed, and the only remaining monuments are some coffins, inscriptions cut on the rocks at the first cataract, at Hammamat and elsewhere, and some stelæ and pieces of sculpture. We must therefore content ourselves with the tombs of officials and of private persons.

THE EXCAVATED TOMBS

At the rise of the XIth dynasty the seat of political power passed from the Delta to Thebes, but some of the finest examples of the tombs of the period are found at Beni-Hassân, about 300 miles north of Thebes. Here, on the eastern side of the Nile, high up on the hills, which approach the river, was excavated out of the solid rock a remarkable series of tombs which open

FIG. 8.

on to a terrace which is common to them all. They contain one or more Halls or Chambers, the last of which is a vestibule to the funeral-chamber and serves the purpose of a "Chamber of Offerings". In many of these tombs the roof is supported by columns cut out of the live rock. The illustration (Fig. 8) shows the funeral-chamber in the tomb of Ameny, a great official of Usertesen I, of the XIth dynasty. At the east end is a narrow niche or shrine, cut far back into the rock, in which was a gigantic seated figure of the deceased. This niche represents the Serdab, and the statue was a Ka figure.

THE PREPARATION OF THE TOMB

The tomb having been excavated by the labourers, it was necessary to prepare the rough walls and make them fit for the work of the painters or carvers.

First came the mason, who smoothed the surface by removing projecting fragments of stone. He cut out all faulty pieces of rock and fitted in sound stone in their place. If it was intended that the scenes and texts were to be carved instead of being painted, the walls were then faced with slabs of suitable stone—

FIG. 9.

hard limestone, or sometimes granite—and then the whole surface was polished. If the walls were to be painted instead of being carved the plasterer followed the mason. He first put on a coating of coarse plaster, which levelled the surface, and finally spread a thin layer of fine plaster, which gave a perfectly even face.

FIG. 10.

An assistant artist then divided the whole surface into squares of exactly equal size by drawing, in black paint, horizontal and vertical lines crossing one another (Fig. 9). These squares were for the guidance of the artist, who afterwards drew in outline the design of the intended picture. All Egyptian paintings were drawn in accordance with conventional rules; the head, the body, the limbs, of a figure, each occupied so many of the square spaces marked on the walls. The chief artist provided a sketch of the picture to be reproduced, which an assistant drew in outline, with red paint, on the squared surface. His work was examined by the master and errors corrected. A good example of this correction is shown by a scene in the palace of Rameses III at Medinet Habû of the king playing at draughts with his wife. The drawing of the king's face and left arm have been corrected, but the faulty lines were not erased (Fig. 10).

As in the Mastabas, so on the walls of the excavated tombs we find representations of the occupations and amusements of daily life on earth. Thus we have agricultural scenes, trades, and entertainments all depicted in lifelike manner. But as we shall see them when we come to the tombs of the XVIIIth and later dynasties, it is better to defer the description of them. In many

FIG. 11.

of the excavated tombs the difficult task of contriving a Serdab in the solid rock was avoided by placing the Ka figures in the chamber with the sarcophagus. The Ka figure here shown (Fig. 11) standing by the sarcophagus was photographed in situ in a XIIth dynasty tomb at Beni-Hassân.

With the close of the XIIth dynasty trouble again arose in Egypt. The invasion by the Hyksos—the Shepherd Kings from

Syria—commenced. The whole country fell into their hands, and the rule of the native Pharaohs ceased. Of this period few, if any, tombs remain in existence. That some at least of the Hyksos Kings were buried in royal style we know from the "Abbott" papyrus, which records the examination, in the XXth dynasty, of the tomb of one of them which was found to have been plundered. The papyrus relates the account, given by one of the thieves, of the objects found in the tomb, which included "amulets and ornaments of gold; the king's body was covered with gold; there were vases of gold, of silver, and of bronze". So we see that the tomb was richly furnished. But nothing of this splendour has come down to us. It was not until Aahmes, the first king of the XVIIIth dynasty, finally drove the Hyksos from their stronghold Avaris, that Egypt was once more ruled by its native kings and the old form of government and religion was restored.

This defeat of the invaders and the rise of the Theban Empire was largely due to the support and assistance given by the priests of Amen-Ra, who were destined to become the most powerful religious community in Egypt. The ruins of their immense Temple at Karnak, built and enriched by a long succession of monarchs, stand as a mighty emblem of the greatness of the Priesthood and the gratitude of the Kings. The power of the priests of Amen extended over all Thebes, on both sides of the Nile, and it is to the tombs excavated in the hills on the western side during the XVIIIth and succeeding dynasties that we shall now direct our attention. The necropolis of Thebes was in the west. As the Sun set in the west and the Sun-god in his boat entered the other world through an opening in the western hills, so men must cross the river to seek on the western side the tomb that was the antechamber to the new life.

THE THEBAN TOMBS

These may conveniently be divided into (1) Royal Tombs and (2) Private Tombs.

(1) THE ROYAL TOMBS. — These are all arranged on much the same plan, and we will therefore take a typical example to illustrate the whole class. The magnificent tomb of Seti I, of the XIXth dynasty, is here shown both in plan and in section (Fig. 12), and will serve our purpose. It commences with a long narrow

flight of stairs and a sloping corridor, followed by another staircase, at the bottom of which is a deep, square well. Beyond this well are a small antechamber and two Halls, the roof of one of them supported by two pillars, of the other by four pillars. To the left of these Halls are passages and small chambers which lead to the great six-pillared Hall and the vaulted chamber in which stood the alabaster sarcophagus of the King, which is now in the Soane Museum. At this point commences a sloping passage which passes into the mountain for a considerable distance, but seems never to have been completed. The total length of the tomb is nearly 500 feet, and the sarcophagus chamber is about 150 feet below the level of the entrance. Now the walls of all these

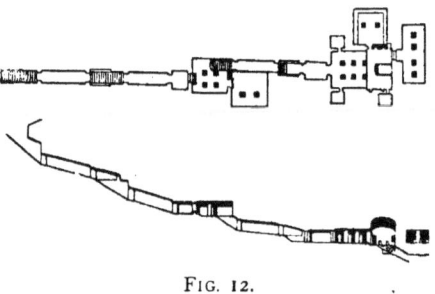

FIG. 12.

corridors and halls are painted, or in some cases carved, with a remarkable series of texts and pictures, which will now occupy our attention.

The Egyptians believed that the "Duat" or other-world was on the same plane as the Earth. The entrance to it was by a cleft in the western range of the chain of mountains which they supposed to be an impassable boundary encircling the whole of Egypt. The further boundary of the "Duat" was a similar mountain range. Thus the "Duat" was a valley extending from west to east, and so forming, with the Sun's path through the heavens, a complete circle. Through it flowed a river, the counterpart of the Nile, which had different names as it passed through the different sections or "Hours" of the night. At sunset each day the Sun-god Ra entered the "Duat" in his boat (Fig. 13), which had neither sails nor rowers, but moved along by magical power. The god stands under a canopy in the centre of the boat, and is accompanied by a number of gods and a goddess, all of whom possess magical "words of power" by which the various obstructions to the passage of the boat are overcome. From the illustration (Fig. 13) it will be seen that the Sun-god has taken the form of a Ram-headed Man, in other words he has taken the form of Osiris, the supreme ruler of the

FIG. 13.

other world. The divisions or "Hours" are divided by gates (Fig. 14), each gate being guarded by a monster serpent which stands erect on its tail, and by Uræi which spat forth streams of fire into the passages between the battlemented walls. Whoever would pass these gates must know the name of the serpent and of

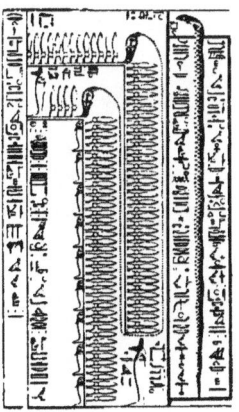

FIG. 14.

every part of the gate, and must, moreover, be possessed of magical "words of power" by which to compel the guardians to give him free passage. This was done for the Sun-god by the god Apuat, "the opener of the ways." When the boat arrives at the third "Hour" it no longer moves without visible aid, but is towed by four gods through a tunnel (Fig. 15) called "the tunnel of the earth", which is borne on the shoulders of eight gods. The tunnel has at each end a bull's head, and the boat with the Sun-god passes completely through it. I believe that this passage through the tunnel refers to burial.

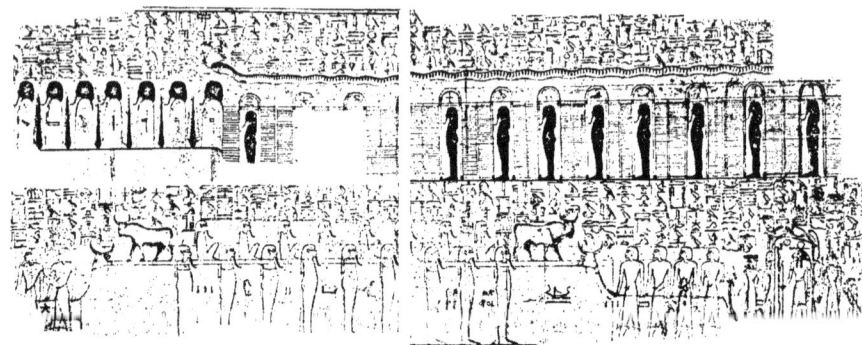

FIG. 15.

And so the Sun-god in his boat passed on through "Hour" after "Hour" until he arrived at the eleventh "Hour", which is the threshold of the dawn. In this division we see the punish-

FIG. 16.

ments awarded to the enemies of Ra. They are marched to judgment with their arms bound behind them (Fig. 16); their heads and shadows and souls are cast into fiery furnaces (Fig. 17), the flames of which are fed by goddesses who spit out endless streams of fire. And now the last opposition to the progress of

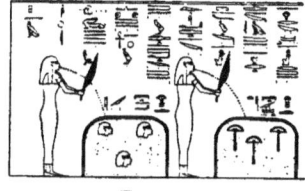

FIG. 17.

Ra is overcome by the capture of the demon serpent Neha-hra, a form of Apep, who is transfixed by knives and held bound by the goddess Serquet and the god Her-tesu-f (Fig. 18). And

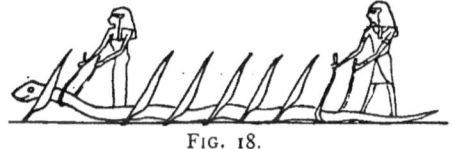

FIG. 18.

finally the Sun-god, under his form as Kheper, transforms himself into the disk of the Sun of daytime which passes through the opening on the eastern side of the wall surrounding the "Duat"

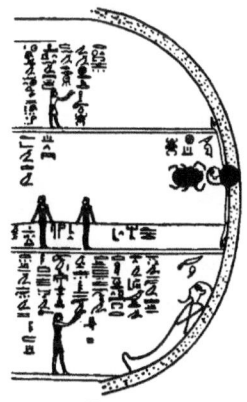

FIG. 19.

and rises once more into the heavens; leaving below him the cast-off body of the Sun of the night—in other words, the Sun rises (Fig. 19).

22 TOMBS OF ANCIENT EGYPT

The above is a mere outline of the story of the Sun-god's progress through the other world. These pictures are accompanied

FIG. 20.

by written texts relating to them, in fact the *Book of Am Duat* is written on the walls of the tomb.

FIG. 21.

But it must be remembered that the cults of Ra and Osiris were more or less confused from early times, and it is seldom that a royal tomb has not some of the scenes from the Osirian's guide-book. Indeed, Seti I, whose tomb we have taken as a model, had a complete copy of the *Book of Gates* carved on his sarcophagus. In the tomb of Hor-em-heb is a drawing of the weighing the heart in the "Hall of the two Truths" (Fig. 20), which of course is purely Osirian.

The scenes described above are for the most part on the walls of the various chambers, but in the corridors we find paintings of a different character. They represent the dead King making offerings to various gods and goddesses, and in return receiving

Fig. 22.

from them promises of protection. Thus we have the King embraced by Nefer-Tum (Fig. 21), and, again, making offerings to Osiris, Isis, and Nepthys (Fig. 22), and many other similar scenes.

Such are the mythological paintings found in a Royal Tomb. In the sepulchral chamber we find numerous objects, the description of which it will be better to defer until after the consideration of the Private Tombs.

(2) THE PRIVATE TOMBS.—I took the tomb of Seti I, of the XIXth dynasty, as a typical example of the royal tombs; I will take the Theban tombs of the XVIIIth dynasty as illustrations of private tombs.

These tombs vary very much in size and in plan, but it by no means follows that the tombs of simplest plan were those of the least important persons. For example, the tomb of Rekhmara, Vezir of Upper Egypt and Governor of Thebes under Thothmes I

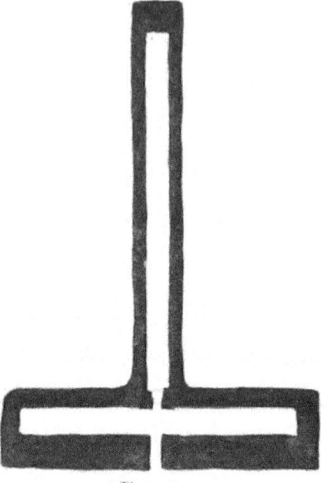

FIG. 23.

and II (Fig. 23), is extremely simple in plan. Entering by a doorway about 9 feet high, the wall being 8 feet thick, we find ourselves in a long, narrow vestibule running right and left of

FIG. 24.

the entrance. In the centre of the further wall of this vestibule is the entrance to a long, narrow passage, the roof of which slopes upwards. At the end, high up, near the roof, is a niche, formerly closed by a "false door", which represents the Serdab. The pit leading to the mummy chamber is in one corner, near the end of the chamber. The whole of the walls and ceilings are painted with scenes recording Rekhmara's official life, and representations of various trades and occupations. As Vezir he had to receive the deputation of the people of Punt (now known to us as Somaliland), bringing tribute to Queen Hatshepsut. The

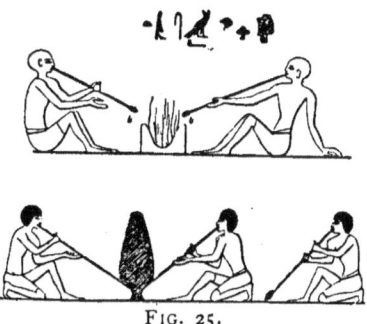

Fig. 25.

illustration (Fig. 24) shows part of the procession of men bringing various gifts of animals, plants, spices, and other things. Among the trades depicted are glass-blowing (Fig. 25), where two men are seated by a fire with long blowing-tubes, each tube having a lump of glass at the end of it, which the workmen are softening in the fire. In the painting the lumps of glass are coloured green.

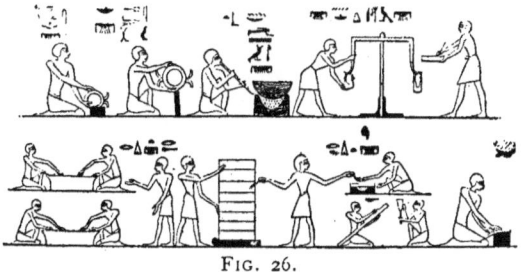

Fig. 26.

Below are two men blowing the softened glass into the form of a bottle. Gold-workers (Fig. 26) are shown at work. . The inscriptions on the upper Register read: (1) "Works the gold." (2) "Works a gold collar.' (3) "Melts the gold." (4) "Gives gold to the scribe of the gold," i.e., Registers the weight of the gold. On the lower Register we have on the left men washing gold. The other inscriptions read: "Gives gold to the superintendent" and "Gives gold to the workmen".

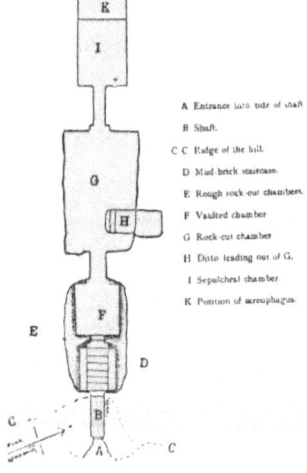

A Entrance into side of shaft
B Shaft.
C C Ridge of the hill.
D Mud-brick staircase.
E Rough rock-cut chambers.
F Vaulted chamber
G Rock-cut chamber
H Ditto leading out of G.
I Sepulchral chamber
K Position of sarcophagus.

FIG. 27.

The tomb of Rekhmara is of unusually simple plan; a more common form is that of the tomb of Pa-shedu (Fig. 27). Here we

FIG. 28.

have a shaft B ending in a flight of steps leading into various passages and chambers which compose the tomb.

As a rule most, if not all, these chambers are richly painted with scenes of social life, and the ceiling coloured with a diaper or chequer pattern. The Stele (Fig. 28) is always present, and bears

FIG. 29.

the usual prayer that abundance of food, etc., may be provided for the benefit of the Ka of the deceased, and on each side are pictured attendants bringing food and wine, while the deceased himself is

FIG. 30.

shown seated at a table enjoying the good things prayed for. At the base of the Stele is represented a table heaped with food (Fig. 29).

Thus we see that the Stele of the XVIIIth dynasty expresses exactly the same ideas as that of the Mastabas, many hundreds of

FIG. 31.

years earlier (see Figs. 5 and 6). Scenes of social life are painted on the walls (Fig. 30), such as guests seated in rows and waited on by attendants. The work on the farm is shown on Fig. 31, where,

FIG. 32.

in the lowest Register, we see the plough drawn by oxen and men sowing the seed; above are the reapers of the standing corn; and on the top Register are oxen treading out the grain and men winnowing it and placing it in a heap. The attending to the cattle and bringing them home from the marshes (Fig. 32) is shown. Trades are depicted, such as those of leather-workers and

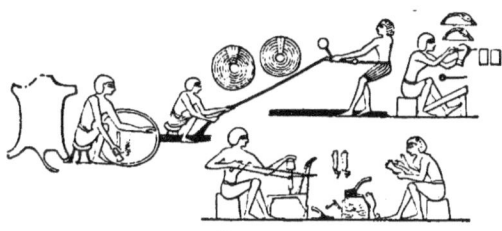

FIG. 33.

carpenters (Fig. 33); on the left is a skin hanging up, indicating the trade; the leather is seen cut into strips and being twisted into thongs, which are then rolled into coils. In the lower part of the

FIG. 34.

same illustration a carpenter is seen drilling a hole in the frame of a chair, while opposite him sits a man polishing the leg of some piece of furniture. Confectioners are seen (Fig. 34) making cakes

FIG. 35.

of various kinds; among them is a sort of macaroni which a man is making on a plate heated by a fire below it, and the finished cakes are shown on the wall above him.

Amusements in abundance are shown. The Egyptian was very fond of fishing, and kept ponds stocked with fish for the purpose. Fig. 35 shows him seated beside a stream, rod in hand. The

FIG. 36.

reader will notice that the water stands, as it were, on edge. This is in accordance with the entire ignorance of perspective which characterizes all ancient Egyptian drawing. Spearing the hippopotamus (Fig. 36) was another favourite form of sport. The picture

FIG. 37.

shows him in the act of throwing the spear while an attendant passes a noose round the animal's neck. Again (Fig. 37), we see our friend amusing himself by fowling. He stands in a boat, in a marsh where tall reeds are growing. In one hand he holds a decoy-duck and in the other is the throw-stick with which he

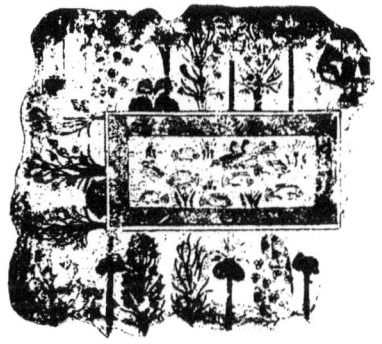

FIG. 38.

knocks down the wild-fowl. The Egyptian was a great gardener also. In Fig. 38 we see one of these gardens, in the centre of

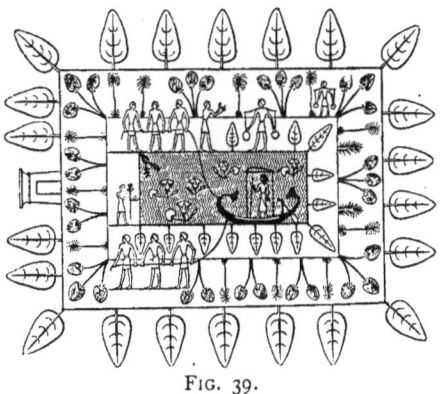

FIG. 39.

which is a lake of water in which ducks and fish are swimming. At other times he enjoyed sitting in a boat which was drawn round the lake by servants (Fig. 39).

FIG. 40.

A game somewhat resembling our game of draughts was universally played, and is constantly depicted (Fig. 40). In the

FIG. 41.

illustration we have two sets of players squatted before draught-boards. The draughtsmen are black and white. Over the board

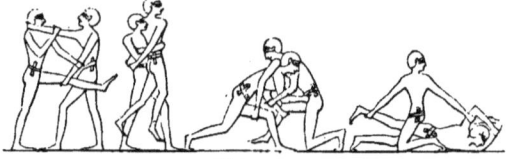

FIG. 42.

on the right is written "To play with five", probably referring to the particular form of the game being played. Over the other board we read "Consumed"—i.e. finished.

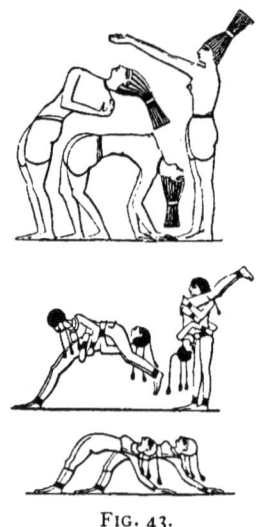

FIG. 43.

Spectacular entertainments also were a favourite amusement: thus we see men dancing to the sound of a drum (Fig. 41); men wrestling (Fig. 42); women performing feats of agility (Fig. 43). Numberless other trades, occupations, and amusements are depicted on the walls of the tombs, but those given will suffice to show the nature of the paintings.

FIG. 44.

In course of time it was found easier and cheaper to deposit in the tombs, either models of many of the objects used in daily life, or even the objects themselves, than to go to the expense of painting pictures of them. Indeed, with regard to many of the things it is highly probable that burying them with the dead *preceded* the adoption of painted representations. But whatever

FIG. 45.

may have been the reason for doing it, it is to this custom that we owe the innumerable objects that are to be seen in every collection of Egyptian Antiquities. Furniture, clothing, weapons, jewellery, tools, models of houses and granaries, everything that was used in life has been found with the dead. Even real boats of great size have been so found, but more often models of them, such as Fig. 44, which is a boat with twenty oarsmen, and Fig. 45,

c

which is a model of the boat in which the mummy was conveyed across the river to the place of burial, and shows the dead man and his wife seated before a table of offerings. Musical instruments (Fig. 46) have been found, both wind instruments and

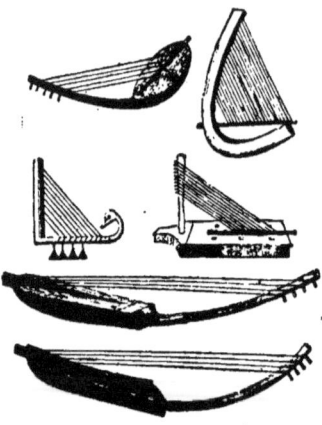

FIG. 46.

various forms of the harp. The children, too, are not forgotten, for their toys, such as dolls and mechanical figures (Fig. 47), were placed in tombs.

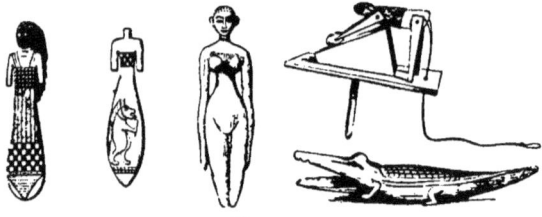

FIG. 47.

In addition to all these objects which belong to the life on earth, there are certain things which are found in all tombs and had a special mythological meaning.

THE KA FIGURES

As in the rock-cut tombs of the XIIth dynasty, so in those of the XVIIIth and later dynasties, the Ka figures were placed in the sarcophagus chamber and not in a Serdab provided for them. They are usually made of wood, often of life-size (Fig. 48), and

FIG. 48.

no doubt were portraits. Very frequently there were several such figures, thus multiplying the Ka's chances of safety.

CANOPIC JARS

Placed in the mummy chamber, generally in a special coffer, were four jars of peculiar shape (Fig. 49). The name "Canopic"

FIG. 49.

was given to them by the early Egyptologists, who saw in them a resemblance to the description, given in the Greek legend, of Canopus, the pilot of Menelaus, who is said to be buried at

Canopus, in Egypt, and was worshipped there under the form of a jar with small feet, a thin neck, a swollen body, and a round back. Each of these jars was dedicated to one of the four deities of the other world, and its lid was carved in the shape of the head of the deity to whom it was dedicated. In the jars were placed the internal organs of the body. Taking them from left to right we have—

Deity.	Contents.	Typified.
Quebsennuf (Hawk-headed)	Liver and Gall-bladder	The West.
Hapi (Cynocephalus)	Small intestines	The North.
Amset (Man-headed)	Stomach and large intestines	The South.
Tuamautef (Jackal-headed)	Lungs and Heart	The East.

THE USHABTI FIGURES

Lastly, buried with the dead were a number of small figures made of faience, of wood, or of stone, and usually in the form of the mummified Osiris. The hands are crossed over the breast, and

FIG. 50.

bear in one a hoe, in the other a flail, or sometimes a hoe in each hand (Fig. 50). On the back is drawn a representation of a basket. The word Ushabti means "Respondent", that is, "one who answers." They are inscribed with the name of the person for whom they were made, and with the sixth Chapter of *The Book of the Dead*, which reads: "Oh! ye Ushabti, if there be any labours to be done by the Osiris in the other world let all obstructions be cast down before him. Be ye ready always to plough and sow the fields, to fill the canals with water, and to carry sand from the east to the west;" to which the Ushabtis reply, "When thou callest here we are." In fact the Ushabtis were servants, who were to do for the deceased all that his servants on earth had done for him.

Such, in general outline, is what we may expect to find in a Theban tomb of a private person. It only remains to explain the meaning and purport of all these sepulchral paintings and objects.

THE MEANING OF THE TOMBS

The Royal Tombs

The priests of Amen-Ra wrote, for the guidance of the worshippers of Ra, what may be called a guide-book to the other-world, called *Am Duat*, that is, the book of that which is in the other world. This book they wrote on papyrus, on coffins, and on the walls of tombs, and they illustrated it with pictures which, as it were, explained and made efficacious the written texts. The paintings depicted the passage of the boat of the Sun through the divisions of the other world, and the written texts gave at full length all the words of power which were essential if the deceased would overcome all the obstacles to his progress and succeed in gaining a passage in the Sun-god's boat, travel with him through the infernal regions, and with him rise again at dawn. Now the efficacy of all these pictures and words of power depended on magic. The paintings and writings were the work of the priests, or done under their direction, in accordance with a strict ritual; and the priests themselves were but the instruments of the gods, especially of the god Thoth, the great god of magic, and the monsters that opposed the progress of the Sun-god and his followers were, by his magical power, coerced by the written words as though they had been spoken. And not only so, by the same magic power the painted scenes and the written words had a real existence. If Apep, the terrible and evil serpent, was pictured transfixed by knives and bound with cords, the picture, by magic, became a reality. If written on the wall, are the magic words that drive back the crocodile fiend Sui, those words are as though they were really spoken and are equally efficacious.

My readers will remember that in the description of the tomb of Seti I, I spoke of scenes, painted in the corridors, which were of a totally different character to those in the Halls and sepulchral chamber. Their meaning is to be found in the ritual of the daily service in the Temples, where the King as head of the priesthood, or his delegate, daily perform the ceremonies of purification; daily he made offerings to the great gods and goddesses of Egypt, and received from them promises of help and protection; daily he restored to the Sun-god, by means of the magical aid of Thoth, the sacred eye which the evil deity Set had snatched away, that he might take the souls of the dead that had fled there for refuge. These ceremonies and their efficacy are, by magical power, transferred to the tomb for the benefit of all who died faithful to the worship of Ra. The tomb was, in fact, a microcosm of the other world, and that which went on in the Temple was for ever renewed there.

The object, then, of the paintings and writings in the royal tomb was to provide the worshippers of Ra with magical aid in becoming one with the god. The King was necessarily, or at least officially, a follower of Ra. From his birth he was declared to be "Sa-Ra"—*Son of Ra*—and therefore it was that his tomb bore, painted on the walls, the Sun-god's progress through the other world, and the magical incantations which enabled his followers, assisted as they were by the Temple service, to overcome all difficulties and finally to rise again with him.

It will be noticed that in all this there is no reference whatever to any life resembling the life on earth. The devout follower of Ra looked for happiness in for ever sailing with Ra in his boat, through the sky by day, through the other-world by night. There is no mention of ploughing or sowing, or of occupations or amusements. The doctrine of Ra included no material life. The sole desire of his worshippers was to become one with Ra, in fact to become beings formed from the light of Ra himself, which was the food on which they subsisted. For what purpose, then, were the Ushabti figures and other objects placed in the royal tomb? The explanation of this inconsistency seems to be that though the Theban Kings, convinced that their military successes were due to the favour of the great Theban God Amen-Ra, dutifully accepted the instructions of his priests in relation to his worship, and allowed them to prepare their tombs in accordance with the tenets of that worship, they never completely threw off their belief in Osiris and his cult. Thothmes III regarded the 154th chapter of the *Book of coming forth by day* (the chapter of not letting the body perish) as all-powerful, and had the whole chapter written on a sheet and wrapped round his body. Seti I had the whole of the book referred to carved on his alabaster sarcophagus. The Kings, in short, determined to omit nothing that was necessary to ensure their eternal happiness, whichever of the cults might be the true one.

The Private Tombs

We have to ask ourselves, what is the meaning of all these scenes of luxury and abundance, these amusements and pleasures, these flocks and herds, these troops of servants? They cannot be meant to represent the life the man led on earth. Such unheard-of affluence could belong to a King only. Moreover, the scenes in all private tombs are of the same character, and are evidently conventional. It seems clear that what they represent is the life hereafter that his friends wished for him.

The priests of Amen-Ra, who wrote the book of *Am-Duat* for the use of the followers of Ra, wrote also a guide-book which they called *Per-em-hru*, that is, *The book of coming forth by day* (or, as it is commonly called, the *Book of Gates*), for the use of the worshippers of Osiris. By the aid of the words of power provided by this book and painted on the walls of the tomb, the deceased arrives at the portal of the kingdom of Osiris, there to be tried by the great judge of the dead in the "Hall of the two Truths". It is here that takes place, under the inspection of Anubis, the weighing of the heart against the emblem of the Goddess of Truth and Justice. The result is recorded by Thoth, and if favourable the deceased is led to Osiris, who bids him enter the "fields of the blessed", there to live for ever a life of material enjoyment. By priestly magic the scenes painted on the walls, the material offerings made by relatives, the frequent funerary sacrifices made on appointed days, all become realities. The "doubles" of the material objects deposited with the dead man pass with him into the other world ; the Ushabti figures become real servants, who plough and sow and reap as they are pictured doing in the tomb. The heaped-up offerings become food, continually renewed, for the life beyond. In short, whatever is pictured, or placed, in the tomb, reappears as a reality in the other world, thanks to the magical incantations of the priests. Throughout the life of the Egyptian, magic by means of amulets and spells was his constant safeguard against evils. From the moment of death it becomes supreme. The perpetual preservation of the body was essential to the eternal life of the Ka, and is ensured by the due performance, in accordance with a strict ritual, of the ceremonies connected with embalmment. Magic words of power are whispered into the dead man's ear. At the entrance to the tomb magic ceremonies are performed which restore to him his powers of speech, of hearing, of movement. And all these magical ceremonies having been duly performed, his friends laid him in the tomb with the certain assurance of his future happiness— a happiness he was to derive from the enjoyment of a perpetual renewal of a life similar to that which he had passed on earth, but freed from all troubles, and vastly more luxurious.

www.ingramcontent.com/pod-product-compliance
Lightning Source LLC
Chambersburg PA
CBHW041929040426
42444CB00018B/3470